EVENING BRINGS EVERYTHING BACK

Jaan Kaplinski was born in Tartu in 1941, shortly after the Soviet occupation of Estonia. His mother was Estonian, and his Polish father died in a labour camp in northern Russia when Jaan was still a child. 'My childhood,' he has said, 'passed in Tartu, a war-devastated university town. It was a time of repression, fear, hypocrisy and poverty.'

Jaan Kaplinski studied Romance Language and Linguistics at Tartu University and has worked as a researcher in linguistics, as a sociologist, ecologist and translator. He has lectured on the History of Western Civilisation at Tartu University and has been a student of Mahayana Buddhism and philosophies of the Far East. He has published several books of poetry and essays in Estonian, Finnish and English, and his work has been translated into Norwegian, Swedish, Latvian, Russian and Czech. Nominated for the Nobel Prize, Jaan Kaplinski published three earlier collections with Harvill in Britain, *The Same Sea in Us All* (1990), *The Wandering Border* (1992) and *Through the Forest* (1996), as well as a book of poems written in English, *I Am the Spring in Tartu*, published in Canada in 1991. His latest book of poems to be published in English is *Evening Brings Everything Back* (Bloodaxe Books, 2004), translated by the author with Fiona Sampson, drawing on three books, *Evening brings everything back* (1984), *Ice and Heather* (1989) and *Summers and Springs* (1995).

He has translated poetry from French, English, Spanish, Chinese and Swedish (a book of poems by Tomas Tranströmer) and travelled in many countries, including Britain, China, Turkey and parts of Russia. Awarded many prizes and honours, he is a member of several learned societies including the Universal Academy of Cultures. Jaan Kaplinski was a member of the new post-Revolution Estonian parliament (Riigikogu) in 1992-95 and his essays on cultural transition and the challenges of globalisation are published across the Baltic region. Further details and texts are on his website at: www.kaplinski.com.

JAAN KAPLINSKI

Evening Brings Everything Back

TRANSLATED BY
JAAN KAPLINSKI
WITH FIONA SAMPSON

BLOODAXE BOOKS

Copyright © Jaan Kaplinski 1984, 1989, 1995, 2004
English translation © Jaan Kaplinski & Fiona Sampson 2004

ISBN: 1 85224 650 2

First published 2004 by
Bloodaxe Books Ltd,
Highgreen,
Tarset,
Northumberland NE48 1RP.

www.bloodaxebooks.com
For further information about Bloodaxe titles
please visit our website or write to
the above address for a catalogue.

Bloodaxe Books Ltd acknowledges
the financial assistance of
Arts Council England, North East.

LEGAL NOTICE
All rights reserved. No part of this book may be
reproduced, stored in a retrieval system, or
transmitted in any form, or by any means, electronic,
mechanical, photocopying, recording or otherwise,
without prior written permission from Bloodaxe Books Ltd.
Requests to publish work from this book
must be sent to Bloodaxe Books Ltd.
Jaan Kaplinski has asserted his right under
Section 77 of the Copyright, Designs and Patents Act 1988
to be identified as the author of this work.

Cover printing by J. Thomson Colour Printers Ltd, Glasgow.

Printed in Great Britain by
Cromwell Press Ltd, Trowbridge, Wiltshire.

CONTENTS

from **Evening brings everything back**
12   The snow's melting...
13   Through the cellar ceiling...
14   White paper and time...
15   For many years, always in March...
16   Voices. Hum of the fridge...
16   Spring has come, gums bleed...
17   It's easy to say what's become of the snow...
17   I was coming from Tähtvere...
18   Once again I think about what I've read...
18   I don't feel at home in this synthetic world...
19   Spring has indeed come...
19   Lilac branches are swaying in the wind...
20   The morning began with sunshine...
21   I could say...
22   Running for milk I saw wood sorrel in bloom...
23   I write a poem every day...
24   We walked the road to Kvissental...
25   As if my lungs couldn't breathe enough...
26   My aunt knew them well...
27   The sky's overcast...
27   It's already dark...
28   Silence is always here...
29   This other life only begins in the evening...
30   I don't want to write courtly poetry any more...
31   Only at dusk do eyes really begin to see...
32   A last cloud moves across the sky...
33   The rain stops...
34   There are so many insects this summer...
35   I don't know whether there was any more in this day...
36   There are as many worlds as grains of sand on a beach...
37   It makes little sense to talk about the subconscious...
38   There is no God...
39   In the town centre, in Vallikraavi Street...
39   The birth of poems remains a mystery...
40   As we humans create literature...
41   The world doesn't consist of matter or spirit...
42   Late summer: a faded old watercolour...
42   The full moon south-east above Piigaste forest...

43   What is essential in poetry?...
43   I told the students about the beginning of Greek culture...
44   From stalks and curls of pine-bark...

Ice and Heather
Notes of a migrant
46   Ice and Heather

from **Summers and Springs**
76   Springs and summers full of song...
77   In the morning I was presented...
77   The radio's talking about the Tiananmen bloodbath...
78   The sea doesn't want to make waves...
78   God has left us...
79   The possibility of rain...
79   A fit body doesn't exist...
80   The age-old dream of mankind...
80   The city's humming, rumbling and buzzing...
81   The ship glides north...
81   The tide's low...
82   One day you will do everything for the last time...
82   I was rinsing laundry at the pond...
83   Evening's coming...
83   It's raining again...
84   The centre of the world is here, in Manchester...
85   The clay god wants to come back...
85   A cloudy afternoon in late autumn...
86   My poems often aren't poems...
86   Less and less space for flying...
87   There are animals who mark their tracks...
87   More and more empty words...
88   The year's half over...
89   I saw something white...
89   The weather changed overnight...
90   My eyesight's weakening...
91   The world is a single event...
91   Through morning dreams...
92   I opened the Russian-Chinese dictionary...
92   It could have been thus...
93   I've thought that I thought about death...
93   Suddenly, everything silent...
94   Tallinn is cold as the whole of Estonia...
94   I don't have a land or a sky of my own...
95   The whole town is covered with ice...

ACKNOWLEDGEMENTS

Evening brings everything back was published as *Õhtu toob tagasi kõik* by Eesti Raamat (Tallinn) in 1984; *Ice and Heather* as *Jää ja kanarbik* by Looming (Tallinn) in 1989; *Summers and Springs* as *Mitu suve ja kevadet* by Vagabund (Tallinn) in 1995.

The translation of 'A fit body doesn't exist' first appeared in Fiona Sampson's *The Healing Word* (Poetry Society, London: 1999). Some of the translations first appeared in *Baltic Poets*, ed. Juris Kronbergs (The Swedish Institute, London: 1999). Acknowledgements are also due to the editors of the following magazines where some of these translations have been published: *Amber, Haiku Quarterly, Interchange, London Magazine, Orient Express, Oxford Poetry, Poetry London* and *Planet*. Six poems from *Summers and Springs* were first published in *Alternatives* 25 (2000): 'Springs and summers full of song...', In the morning I was presented...', 'The radio's talking about the Tiananmen bloodbath...', 'The sea doesn't want to make waves...', 'God has left us...' and 'The possibility of rain...'

Special thanks are due to Arts Council England for providing a translation grant for this book.

Hespere panta fereis hosa fainolis eskedas auos
fereis oin fereis aiga fereis apy materi paida

Evening, you bring back everything the bright dawn scattered:
bring back the ewe, bring back the kid, bring the child back to its mother.

SAPPHO

Ehatähte, hella tähte,
see viib värvud välla pealta,
aab haned aruninasta,
vanad vaipa ju vautab,
noored nurka uinutelleb.
Koidutähte, kurja tähte,
see viib värvud välla peale,
vanad vaibast erutab,
noored nurgast kergitelleb.

Evening star, tender star,
takes the little birds from the field,
takes the geese from the meadow,
puts the old under a blanket,
the young to sleep in the corner.
Morning star, cruel star,
chases the little birds to the field,
gets the old out of bed
raises the young from the corner.

ESTONIAN FOLK SONG

I

FROM
Evening brings everything back

The snow's melting. Water's dripping.
The wind's blowing, gently.
Boughs sway. There's a fire in the stove.
The radiators are warm.
Anu is doing exercises on the piano.
Ott and Tambet are making a snowman.
Maarja's preparing lunch.
The wooden horse is looking in at the window.
I am looking out of the window.
I am writing a poem.
I'm writing that today is Sunday.
That the snow's melting. That water's dripping.
That the wind's blowing, *et cetera*, *et cetera*.

*

> *Zwei Dinge erfüllen das Gemüt mit immer neuer und
> zunehmender Bewunderung und Ehrfurcht, je öfter und
> anhaltender sich das Nachdenken damit beschäftigt: der
> gestirnte Himmel über, und das moralische Gesetz in mir.**
> KANT

Through the cellar ceiling
I hear the shouts of children,
their feet trampling, sometimes
a building block falling and sometimes
their mother's nagging voice.
Above these voices there are
more ceilings,
the roof with chimneys and aerials,
and heaven actually begins
here at this very place
beside us, around us
and reaches up to those
awe-inspiring stars.
We too are heaven-dwellers,
the contemplative philosopher
as well as a child throwing its wood blocks onto the floor
and the writer who doesn't know
whether he feels more awe
for the stars in heaven, castles built of wood blocks,
or the heavenly sandstone
outside the cellar walls and below its floor.

*

---

* 'Two things fill the spirit with renewed and ever greater admiration
and awe the more often and the more sustainedly we reflect upon them.
They are: the starry sky above me and the moral law within me.'

— KANT (*trs. David Constantine*)

White paper and time: I'm filling one,
the other fills itself.
Both so similar. In front of both
I am shy and full of awe.
The poem is like a sheep
in a dark shed with a high threshold.
I feel uneasy when I approach it.
Sight stays outside. Here you can move
only with the help of your hands.
White paper. White wool. In the dark
both simply something not dark. Time
both invisible and visible
as it is outside in broad daylight
where you left your eyesight.
Time: a white wet towel. Poetry trickling out
when you twist it.
The towel drying on a warm pipe
in a dark bathroom.

*

For many years, always in March,
I've felt sorry for these quiet
days and cloudy skies. The arrival
of the real spring has something
frightening in it. Everything
is suddenly new and strange: the doormat, unwashed windows,
willow buds, tufts of grass sticking up through the snow,
the starlings and the moon above the floodplain.
Everything is like a call, everything's tempting and luring you
out of the room, out of home, out of yourself, out of mind;
to flow over land and water, to go somewhere else,
to be somewhere else, somebody else;
and if you cannot then at least
to shout, to dance, to write,
to sing stupid spring songs
in order to soothe this urge.
I can't understand whether it's in the blood or the mind
or somewhere else. Maybe it's the cellular memory
of my ancestors – fish, birds or peasants –
the memory of previous lives awakening in me
an urge to swim to flooded meadows to spawn
to look for a partner and a nesting place
to feel with a hand whether the soil is warm enough;
or something even more mysterious and archaic:
the understanding of a seed that it's time to sprout,
the thrill and fear of yet another death and birth.

*

Voices. Hum of the fridge. Squeak of the door.
Steps on stairs. Water in the pipes. A kind of rumbling
probably at the neighbours'. The scrape of a chair on the floor.
The click of the switch. Distant roar of an engine: a plane
or a big lorry on the road. Then the footsteps of our boys
in the first floor room. Water running. Some creaks
you don't even recognise. All these
belong to our home, our
everyday background of sounds that's
ebbing now, leaving space
for something more silent and deep:
for this sound in your ears, like
the hum of high-voltage lines above the clearing in summer,
that brings to mind bracken, thyme
and wild strawberries, strawberries
rising before my closed eyes as they did once long ago.

*

Spring has come, gums bleed,
eyes are sore from light
that's reflected by the last patches of snow
and the polytunnels. The eye picks out
buds on the poplars behind the allotments, and further away
ducks splashing in glittering water.
Already the children go cycling,
come home dirty, with bruised knees,
but even they get tired early and sleep long:
hours of silence, measured by the clock
ticking in front of the Latin Anthology
and the sound of water trickling through the climbers.

*

It's easy to say what's become of the snow
where we went skiing only two weeks ago,
upstream, past the ruins of Jänese tavern and the railway bridge
where on both sides
there's only forest: alder and birch
slanting towards the water, earthworks on both banks
probably left by dredging.
I could say: the snow's gone, melted, flowed
into Peipsi lake and further away, evaporated, soaked into soil.
But I still think of those ski tracks,
of our traces on the snowy river ice...
What have they become? Do such traces
vanish completely, without leaving any traces? And are we
like that snow or those ski tracks?
Or like neither of them? Something different, something else?

*

I was coming from Tähtvere. It was Sunday evening.
I was the only fare to the final stop.
I stepped out. The road was silent: not a single car.
The wind had fallen silent. Only the stars
and the sickle of the new moon shone above the river.
I felt sorry I had to keep going. I'd have liked to step
off the path onto the wasteland and to stop
to look at that moon, those constellations – several of which
I'd forgotten again during the winter – but most of all
at the sky itself, the blue of the sky that was nearly
as deep and strange as once long ago,
twenty years ago, when we sat and drank wine
around a campfire in the nearby forest, and I came
back to Tartu on a village road with a girl,
arms around each other's necks.
The blue is much easier to remember
than names, titles or faces,
even the faces of those you once loved.

*

Once again I think about what I've read: that light and darkness,
good and evil, truth and lies, are mixed up in this world. Certainly
for those who thought like that the world really was alive: everything
was black or white, God's or the Devil's own.
But what will remain of this world split into two camps
if everything becomes infinitely divisible, crumbles
into a whirlwind of particles, flickering of fields?
Will every particle contain some dark and light,
will the opposites be there even in the tiniest of them,
even in zero itself, splitting what is closer and closer
to non-existence? Will the strange
replace the horrible? Will it be easier
to exist?

*

I don't feel at home in this synthetic world
where the good old varnish smell is replaced
by the whiff of acrylic and glyphtal paints
I find it hard, sometimes impossible, to get accustomed to;
where shelves and tables are made of sawdust
and you can play the *Ode to Joy* on a plastic flute
or listen to it in a recording
by some long-dead conductor. Your environment
consists of dead things, people and voices. Life withdraws
in front of us, until there's only wilderness to retreat to.
Or it survives in hideouts beside us:
in flower-pot, aquarium, wall crack, dustbin.
A student awake late at night
puts the book aside and kills some bedbugs
which, as always, leave their holes at a certain hour
and creep into the bed.

*

Spring has indeed come: the willows are in blossom and queen
    bumblebees
are looking for nesting places; fruit flies circle
over the bowl of sour milk; on the kitchen curtain
a big moth's sleeping exactly on a red spot.
A mosquito flies into the cellar room and buzzes around my head.
For some time, sitting at the desk, I've been hearing
a strange noise from a plastic sachet hanging on the wall.
Finally I take it down and have a look: a spider
has fallen into it and is making desperate attempts to get out.

*

Lilac branches are swaying in the wind
and shadows creep across the floor from the open balcony door,
swaying too. Today I washed the windows
and was sad for a long time: suddenly everything
was so close by, so clear, so much here and now,
that my own being distant became more evident,
more desolate. Is it really only in a late autumn
forest that I've met friends: great-tits and spruce?
Have I met myself there? Where does this sadness come from?
The sun moves on. The wind dies down.
The shadows of the lilac branches keep swaying on the bookshelf
before vanishing.

*

The morning began with sunshine – we brought the rugs out
to be aired, sent the children to the sand pit
and ourselves went to the garden where
the dandelions and couch grass were already rampant, the
    strawberry bed
full of flowering corn mint buzzing with bumblebees.
We had to clear everything up, dig the whole patch,
tear out couch grass, horsetail and bindweed root by root.
It took a lot of time. Surely later on
it will be nice to think that we've gone through every bit of soil
with our fingers. In the early afternoon
it was so hot that I even took my shirt off, digging. In the west
clouds were gathering already, and in late afternoon,
when the first beds were ready, it began to rain.
I sowed carrots and turnips
when it was already raining, with my black waterproof on.
At night, before falling asleep, I saw
only earth and roots, roots, roots.

*

I could say: I got out of the bus,
stepping onto the dusty verge where
a young maple and a wild rose grow.
In reality, I jumped into silence
and there was no ground to step on.
The silence closed over my head like water:
I barely noticed the bus leaving
and as I sank deeper and deeper
I heard only my own heartbeats,
seeing the way home glide past
in its own rhythm: lilies of the valley sprouting,
wood sorrel already nearly in blossom,
the anthill covered as if by a brownish quivering veil –
the ants themselves. The Big Pine. The Big Spruce.
Drying hurdles. Sand pit. Traces of a fire.
White birch trunks. The Big Boulder.
And many memories. Silence, the inland sea,
nameless background of all these names,
of all our names.

*

Running for milk I saw wood sorrel in bloom
to the left of the path, and my mind became restless,
feeling its helplessness in front of something primeval and strange
that occasionally – but furtively, evasively –
touches you. In a forest in spring
I feel like a prisoner who has nothing more
than the walls of his cell, scribbled full of words and names,
and memories of free space, landscapes, women
and thirst for all of them. What is there
between me and the forest, between me and the world?
Where is the wall that keeps me apart
from what everything in me thirsts for, the wall
that separates me from this wood sorrel,
these horsetails, cow wheat, wintergreens, from this sprouting
that I must always walk past, that I can never
really touch...? But still – this time
a new thought woke in my besieged mind –
maybe all the time I've sought and longed for
a reality behind this reality; trying to get closer
I've gone further away. For the first time
I understood that transparency itself is nothing less
than what you see through it: the evening sun
shining through petals of wood sorrel.

*

I write a poem every day,
although I'm not quite sure if these texts
should be called poems at all.
It's not difficult, especially now
when it's spring in Tartu, and everything is changing its form:
parks, lawns, branches, buds and clouds
above the town, even the sky and stars.
If only I had enough eyes, ears and time
for this beauty that sucks us in like a whirlpool
covering everything with a poetic veil of hopes
where only one thing sticks out unnaturally:
the half-witted man sitting at the bus stop
taking boots from his dirty maimed feet,
his stick and his woollen cap lying beside him;
the same cap that was on his head
when you saw him that day standing
at the same stop at three in the morning
as the taxi drove you past him and the driver
said, 'That idiot's got hold of some booze again.'

*

We walked the road to Kvissental,
blooming bird cherries on both sides
white clouds of blossom in the midst of a willow thicket.
I broke off a twig of blossom for my son
and showed him the willows: one had vivid green,
the other greyish leaves. 'But why do the willows exist?'
he asked, and it was difficult to find an answer.
I told him the trees simply exist without knowing
or thinking anything. He probably didn't understand
my idea. But how can I speak
for trees? We reached the river.
We went to the old jetty that was swaying
in waves from passing motor boats;
we sat on an old beam, seeing how glittering blue
this river was, which in the north passes through forest;
seeing how dandelions, buttercups and ash
were germinating in the dirt between the pier planks.
We caught some caddis worms and put them back in the river;
we washed our sweaty and dusty faces
in the greenish flowing water, and began our trip back home.

*

As if my lungs couldn't breathe enough
of your air, spring in Tartu, as if my eyes couldn't
see enough of you, as if my feet couldn't walk enough
in the old streets on the other side of the river:
lilac in courtyards, young grass between cobblestones and slabs,
a young birch that has demolished
a thick wall: the stones are lying there in a heap
around its victorious roots and nobody's
clearing them, putting them back.
Some houses seem abandoned here
by another time and life: a plastered wall, an iron gate
and a tree of life at the entrance. A small pond
already nearly covered by duckweed,
as every summer. Another wall and behind it,
in the humid shadow of maples and linden trees,
goutweed, touch-me-not, chickweed, burdock
and under them and under stone slabs
the rich black soil mingling with what remains of those
whose names few can still read:
H-a-n-n-a L-i-b-e-s-m-a-n... D-a-v-i-d...

*

My aunt knew them well. I know
only their names and what other people have told me:
tinkers, haberdashers, attorneys, doctors,
Genss, Michelson, Itzkowitsch, Gulkowitsch...
Where are they now? Some of them were lucky enough
to be buried in this cemetery under a slab with Hebrew lettering.
But those my aunt met on the streets of German-occupied Tartu,
with a yellow star sewn to their clothes, and to whom
she even dared to speak to the horror of her friends:
they are not here, they are scattered
into nameless graves, ditches and pits
in many places, many countries, homeless in death
as in life. Maybe some of them are hovering
in the air as particles of ash, and have not yet
descended to earth. I've thought
that if I were a physicist I would like to study dust,
everything that's hovering in the air, dancing in sunlight,
getting into eyes and mouths, into the ice of Greenland
or between the books on the shelf. Maybe one day
I would have met you,
Isaac, Mordechai, Sarah, Esther, Sulamith
and whoever you were. Maybe even today I breathed in
something of you with this intoxicating spring air;
maybe a flake of you fell today on the white white
apple blossom in my grandfather's garden
or on my grey hair.

*

The sky's overcast. The warm wind creeps under your shirt.
A spotted cat walks slowly towards the dusk.
Dusk moves slowly towards the spotted cat.
A neighbour's wife is taking clothes from the line.
I don't see her, I only see the clothes vanishing
one by one. I see the white lilac.
Narcissi and carnations. And lights
shining far away on the other side of the river. One recorder.
One radio. One reed warbler. And many,
many nightingales.

*

It's already dark, but I can still see
black on white, although the poem
lingers in coming. My senses are full of
green, the lush big green
of our lawn, grass up to my waist,
cow parsley and dandelions I mowed
the whole afternoon; full of ash and elm,
of the cork tree, honeysuckle and the guelder rose
crowded with caterpillars who'd gnawed its leaves
into withering lace. What remained
of the flowering bush was only bare black twigs
on a green background. Almost like this poem here.

*

Silence is always here and everywhere;
sometimes we simply hear it more clearly:
fog covers the meadow, the barn door is open,
a redwing's singing over there, a white
moth circles incessantly around the elm branch
and the branch itself is still swaying imperceptibly
against the background of the evening sky.
The dusk robs us all of faces and names,
only the difference between light and dark remains.
The heart of a midsummer's night:
the old watch on the desk
is suddenly ticking so terribly loudly.

*

This other life only begins in the evening
when the wind dies down, the clouds
gather on the horizon waiting for tomorrow
and the aroma of honeysuckle is flooding
courtyard and garden.
The heron alights at the pond and stays still
waiting. Through the bird cherries
I see something light close to the water,
and somehow it is hard to believe it's anything other
than just a spot of bright evening sky
reflected on the still surface whose peace
is disturbed only by some water insect
or a line drawn by the dorsal fin
of a carp.

*

I don't want to write courtly poetry any more,
the poetry of a horseman who sees the world only
from the eyeholes of my helmet
and in whose mind and language the horse-trot has left
its indelible *tata-rata, tata-rata,*
and who's always racing over and past everything.
In my life and poetry I've always wanted
to be a pedestrian, a wandering scholar who can
sit down on every hillside that's to his liking,
look at everything he wants to,
look at the bumblebee who searches
each blossom of the red clover in turn
and then follow it with his eyes until it vanishes
in the blue of the summer sky; to stay for a while
without thinking, just like that,
enjoying all this transient beauty
until the cool shadow of a cloud
falls upon me, reminding me
that it's time to stand up and go: evening
is approaching, I must find accommodation somewhere
and tomorrow at daybreak start again, to reach
the town before the gates close.
Maybe I'll find some work there
writing letters, composing verse
and teaching Latin to boys (and even girls)
of the better families.

However, a reminiscence of this hillside, this bumblebee
and this shadow of a cloud will remain, and will sometimes
sound in the background of my songs about summer,
about birds singing and, of course, about Venus
and some buxom tavern-maid who was ready
to share with a poor scholar, free, just for a song he made,
what they call love. Yes
in one of my songs I spoke of the bumblebee
on the red clover-blossom and of the cool shadow
of the cloud on the face of the wanderer
who suddenly thought he didn't know
how to write about it all in Latin... And now,
seven hundred years later, all I remember
are these lines:

*Qualis in aestivo sudo
nova, mira pulchritudo
subito in omnibus*

*rebus, avibus, insectis;
novis, laetis et perfectis
patet mundus sensibus.*

*

Only at dusk do eyes really begin to see.
The colours of flowers become lucid and bright
before night extinguishes them: carnations, yellow roses,
meadow-vetch and buttercups.
The wind has died down and the sky
– the faded, nearly invisible
background of all our comings and goings –
is suddenly here, just above the treetops and pylons,
shining through foliage and above the roof of the house
in all its depth and blueness. Behind the outhouse
Venus appears; to the right of the pole of the well, Jupiter:
once two gods, now two stars.

*

A last cloud moves across the sky from west to east.
A last bee alights on the flight board of the hive.
A last bird flies over the garden into the spruce hedge.
I see only its hurrying silhouette
against the background of the sky, and a swaying branch
there where it vanished. Has it a nest there?
The voice of the corncrake comes nearer and nearer.
Now it's just behind the fence. Another crake
answers it from the roadside field. Maybe
they will meet one another tonight. Maybe tomorrow night.

*

The rain stops and, for an instant, the sun emerges from clouds.
The shadow of the pen appears on the white paper.
A redwing is singing somewhere. The wind rises
and raindrops roll off the leaves of the honeysuckle.
They say I haven't written as suggestively as in my youth,
in the book *Of dust and colours*. The sun
casts a yellowish light on the quivering green world
and vanishes once again behind a cloud. I remember
that I must make a roof for the empty beehive
where the wasps nested. In the autumn I must trim down
some apple tree branches growing in front of the loft door
that are a nuisance when we want to put hay in the loft. Also
I should wash some used preserve cans:
they're good for nails or to mix paint.
For the first time I try seriously to write a poem.
It's in Russian. It begins like this:

Nad...i mrachnym Baikalom
odinokaya chayka letit...

Isn't it suggestive?
There is a time for everything. At the gate
the water ash, *Ptelea trifoliata*, is in bloom
and the rye stalks are already rustling dry.

*

There are so many insects this summer.
As soon as you go into the garden
a buzzing swarm of flies besieges you.
The bumblebees are nesting in boxes you made for birds,
the wasps have made their nests in hazel bushes.
And sitting at your desk in the attic room
you constantly hear a buzzing, and don't know
whether it's the sound of bumblebees, wasps,
electric wires,
a plane in the skies, a car on the road,
or the voice of life itself wanting to tell you something
from the inside, from your inner self.

*

I don't know whether there was any more in this day
than in the others that, in my memory, turn into a mess
like over-ripe raspberries in the bowl.
In the morning we had sunshine, the kids could go
naked into the sandpit and to mother in the garden.
I nailed cement plates to the roof, reaching the chimney,
and fastened planks to the rooftop.
We topped and tailed the gooseberries,
dug the first new potatoes. We went with Lemmit to the shop,
discovering that they were out of sugar: everybody making jam.
I borrowed our neighbour's tractor and brought home
some logs and poles from a fallen down shed.
I thought of two other neighbours who, in a couple of days,
would go to court. One has claimed
the other lets his children throw pieces of steel wire
onto his pasturage. If it's true (I think
it's not impossible at all), a big step
toward the escalation of conflict
has been taken here, in the hinterland of Tartumaa,
and unwillingly I think how lucky we are
that our neighbours live so far away.
I was about to write these lines several times already, but my mind
was restless, I don't know why. At the window, in the honeysuckle
      bushes,
thrushes were picking the last berries. The radio said
that a US Navy task force
was approaching the Nicaraguan coast.
Slowly, the sky became overcast, and at night,
when the children were already asleep, it started to rain.
Listening to the raindrops falling I felt my mind calming down
and the past day taking on a form, becoming a series of things
      that happened.

*

There are as many worlds as grains of sand on a beach.
Big and small, round and square,
light and dark, age-old and transient:
some stand still, some go round,
some are alone, some in swarms;
and in every one of these big and small,
round and square, light and dark,
age-old and transient worlds there are seas and beaches,
and plenty of sand on those beaches;
and in each grain of sand there are as many worlds
as grains of sand on a beach, big and small,
round and square. In some of them
Buddha is already born, on some of them
he's not yet born, in some of them
he is living and teaching just now.
In one of them I'm sitting at my desk in the attic room
and a wood warbler, *Phylloscopus sibilatrix*,
flies up to my window, so I can see close up
the yellow stripe above its dark eye
and how it knocks with its beak
on the window-pane and then flies away.

*

It makes little sense to talk about the subconscious,
maybe even about consciousness itself:
there are no borders, no ground, there's nothing
to stand on. I have a mind and a face,
but the mind and face have no me.
Everything reaches everything: it's at once
both conscious, subconscious and unconscious
and everything else. But what, then,
is all that stuff with so many names: anger, pain,
anxiety, sadness? Even being angry, being in pain:
I can't believe they really exist.
What could we compare them to in this floating world?
With the wind coming and going, with waves;
with cracks, an invisible line without breath
running though this beautiful midsummer evening.
If everything is in everything then maybe
in this everything are even the things
that separate everything from everything:
cracks, lines, borders... barbed wire
on which every spring a whinchat sings
and where tufts of goats' or lambs' wool flutter in the breeze.

*

There is no God,
there is no director,
there is no conductor.
The world makes itself happen,
the play plays itself,
the orchestra plays itself.
And if the violin drops from somebody's hand
and their heart stops beating
the man and his death never meet:
there's nothing behind the glass;
the other side is nothing, is just a mirror
where my own fear regards me
with big eyes.
And behind this fear,
if only you look carefully enough,
there are grass and sunflowers
turning slowly by themselves towards the sun
without a God, a director, a conductor.

*

In the town centre, in Vallikraavi Street,
I saw a lonely ant pulling a blade of grass across the hot asphalt.
I went to the Art Gallery and, wiping sweat from my forehead,
looked at Mari Kaarma's watercolours of crows in winter.
I had little time and lots of things to carry in my backpack:
a kilo of noodles, a kilo of rice, a kilo of beans and a can of grey paint;
I had to subscribe to journals for next year,
pick some tomatoes from the greenhouse,
buy – if I could find any – some meat and sausages
before taking the bus back to our country home.
I met several friends, heard some news,
but what I remember now of this trip to town
is that lonely ant on dusty empty hot asphalt.

*

The birth of poems remains a mystery.
Sometimes it seems to be a kind of awakening
although it's difficult to say from what:
the day, life, personality, 'ego', all this
is then like a waking sleep
that's suddenly broken so you catch a glimpse
of something purely accidental, immaterial: two grass-stalks
on the stairs shifting in the wind, a birch leaf
lying on the sauna floor, light refracted
sideways through my wife's iris
and, behind all this, late summer heat, the sound of faraway thunder,
the shrieks of buzzards overhead
and the trembling voice of grasshoppers
that can't be compared to anything else. You see everything
in a mirror, everything suddenly
resembles the face looking at you
from the other side of the mirror.

*

As we humans create literature
literature creates us, casts us in bronze
and puts us on a high pedestal: makes somebody a poet.
From below you can see
only the noble profile, open shirt (bronze),
and gaze fixed on the far woods and the dump.
I've been there: it's a nasty place to stay
for days and nights, in heat and cold
pretending your face and body don't care at all
about the admirers and the envious staring at you
and God's birds shitting on your head.
I've been a poet, I know
more about myself than those people
who understand only my poems of youth
– *Oh death pure as a spring,*
land where we'll all meet –
and in whose imagination I was turning
into a Poet, a Jaan-on-a-pedestal.
In reality I've broken all ten commandments,
many written and unwritten laws,
rules of grammar and rules of poetry.
I like sex more than ethics and aesthetics
I like women more than high ideals
I like children more than women
and my own skin is dearer to me than nation or culture.
I'm nearly the statistical average,
a comet among comets, one in a long catalogue;
one of those who as they approach the sun
can unfold their tail, consisting mainly of dust, only once
before they vanish into empty space, carrying with them
a lot of spent energy.

*

The world doesn't consist of matter or spirit,
of fields, particles or dynamic geometry.
The world consists of questions and answers,
the world is *wen-do* or *kong-an*
(in Japanese *mondo* and *koan*). Today at noon
a relative of mine drove up in his jeep
and told me that next Thursday I have to go to a funeral:
V.'s twelve-year-old son fell
from the stable-loft onto a concrete floor
and died two days later without regaining consciousness.
I know this too is a question.
I know there's an answer here. I know
I should know the answer but...

*

Late summer: a faded old watercolour
more and more lacking in colour and depth.
As every autumn, big clumsy flies
creep through cracks into rooms
and can't find the way out. In the evening clouds gather
in the sky but there's not even a dew at night. Jays
pick the last peas from the bed.
Flocks of thrushes light on rowan trees.
We've seen it so many times already. The long drought
has left its imprint on our faces and thoughts.
And it's hard to believe there's anything new
under the sun, except the wind and some delusory clouds,
meteor-flashes in the night sky and other
accidental things that you for some reason
take notice of and keep in mind, like the earwig
that turned around and around on the gravel path
beside our house.

*

The full moon south-east above Piigaste forest.
A ripe apple falling with a thump
from the crab-apple tree behind the privy.
Two round things calling to my mind
Chinese poetry and the round teaching
of hua-yen philosophy: every single thing
contains all other things,
as I have several times thought and said,
and cannot but think and say once again,
tonight, some nights before the autumn equinox.

*

What is essential in poetry? Neither form nor content,
neither tradition nor innovation. Neither poetics
nor education nor its absence. You just have to keep in mind
the meaning of the word 'inspiration' – breathing in –
and its counterpart 'expiration' – breathing out.
Breathing: the beginning and end of meditation.
For some people it's natural and easy,
for some it's not. Breathing from second to second
liberates you from the spinning of your mind – *cittavrtti* –
giving you back your body, your presence and your present tense,
and the Big Lull where a hundred flowers and scholars burst into
      bloom
and a hundred poems, clouds and rivers are born.

*

I told the students about the beginning of Greek culture.
Telling them the Hittite story of Ullikummi I said
that among known Lydian inscriptions there are some
poetic texts, but they can hardly be read. I also talked about Homer
and his gods, about the tomb of Zeus on Crete
and the religion of Mithra which proclaims
that the world is a battleground of two mighty adversaries –
the forces of Good and Evil, Truth and Lie, Dark and Light –
and the faithful are Mithra's soldiers, the soldiers of Light
in this age-old war where stone stands against stone,
tree against tree, animal against animal, man against man.
Then I finished and took the bus home.
I was tired and had a terrible thirst.

*

From stalks and curls of pine-bark
the flycatcher builds its nest.
From gravel and pebbles
the glaciers have built hills and drumlins.
From short poems
I put together my own China:
it's so easy to walk and breathe
in your company,
Tao Yuanming, Li Bo, Meng Haoran.

II

Ice and Heather

ICE AND HEATHER

Notes of a migrant

❃

I have gathered and brought home stones from everywhere. From Saaremaa. From Armenia. From Ireland. From British Columbia. In Armenia I even wrote a poem, the only poem in Russian I have ever written: 'Stikhi ob armyanskom kamne'. When I had to propose a toast, I proposed it to the Armenian rock. Rock becomes sand, sand becomes soil, and out of soil grow the food and wine that has made Armenians Armenian. A writer from Leninakan (now called Gyumri) promised he would try to publish my poem in an Armenian translation. I don't know whether he did, I don't even know what became of him and the other people I met in that town, after the big earthquake hit Armenia and the city of Leninakan turned into a heap of rubble like my native city in an old lament written, after the Nordic war, in my native dialect.

❃

There are many stones in Armenia but I had little time for them, as always on my trips. On one occasion I simply asked the driver to stop for a while: so I was able to leave the car and take a few steps on the mountain to look for stones.

❃

In fact, Armenia is made entirely of stone, it is one huge rock, a rocky island amidst the Middle East, a mass grave in history. Armenian stone crosses – hackars – resemble the Irish ones. Armenia itself resembles Ireland. Ireland too is an island, a rocky island. From there I brought home pebbles I'd gathered on the beach, and some shells. The others went to have lunch. I felt I couldn't go, I wanted to walk on the beach and look for stones. It was low tide, and I found several nice pebbles and shells. It was on the open Atlantic shore, in one of the westernmost places of Europe, where the sun sets into the ocean, and the souls of the dead set off on a journey across it, according to the belief of the ancient Celts and probably of their modern descendants too.

❋

I have been to Lapland twice. The first time was when we had just married. Tiia was expecting, but nevertheless she came on the trip. She was young, tough and happy. We crossed mountain passes and collected stones: white flintstones with black-and-yellow patches of lichen on them. I haven't seen such lichen anywhere else. One stone weighed several kilos. It was lost when we moved to another flat; we still have the other, smaller one.

❋

In Lovozero, *Luuiavr* in the Saami language, we met some Saamis. Most of them were drunk. The Russians and Komis laughed at the small Saamis tottering around the shop. We visited a home where we met two old women who sang for us. One of them sang her personal song, her *Schicksalslied*, as it is called in ethnographic literature, and then burst in tears.

❋

Here in Estonia the rock bottom, the mother rock, lies deep underground. The stones one can find here – pebbles, slingstones, boulders – don't have their origins here. They come from elsewhere, from Finland, from Sweden, from Lapland. Even the sandstone and clay have their origins there, in the mountains of Fennoscandia from where the Devonian rivers carried them here. Sand itself comes from there, as does the soil. We too are a result of the persistent toil of eroding, Neptunian forces. We are Neptunian nations, probably different from the Plutonian nations whose homeland is a playground of chthonic forces on the shores of the Mediterranean, in Armenia and elsewhere.

❄

One of the most famous buildings of my native town Tartu was the Stone Bridge, a bridge made of hewn granite boulders. It was a gift from the Empress Catherine to the town when it had been devastated by fire. In the age of the automobile the old narrow bridge was no longer any good for traffic, but a bus route was still able to cross it. In 1941, when the German army approached Tartu, retreating Russians dynamited the bridge. People say that the boulders were sealed with lead; in order to melt it, they burned heaps of firewood on it for a day and a night. The quantity of explosives was so great that the boulders were slung over the whole town centre. Some were still to be seen on the pavements when I was a little child. Later they were taken away. Probably they were ground into gravel. It's said that, although before the explosion people were evacuated from the vicinity, the military forgot about a man working nearby in a small pumping station. Both the building and the man survived, but he was deafened by the blast. It is also said that the explosion killed some people. I have heard of only one such case that seems certain: a woman who was hurrying home across the bridge never arrived.

❄

At the same time as the bridge was blown up, 192 prisoners the authorities had no time to evacuate were killed. Among them was Leo, a nephew of my mother's. He was arrested by pure chance: he happened to be at a neighbour's when the NKVD came to arrest the man. Leo was taken too. Later the bodies of the murdered people were brought out of the prison well and lime pit. This was done by new prisoners: real and suspected communists, some of whom were later executed in their turn. It is said that the bodies found in the well and especially those in the lime pit were so disfigured that some were identified only by their clothing.

❄

We bought this old farmhouse nineteen years ago. Its last inhabitant was an old bachelor who slept and cooked his food in the kitchen: the other rooms weren't heated, and the floors there had begun to decay. The range didn't draw, the ceiling was sooty and full of cobwebs. There were no flowers close to the house, only some big ash trees and lilacs growing nearby. The fences were falling down, the roofs leaked. On the first evening I understood that I had to begin repairing, mending and adjusting the fences, roofs, floors, pipes, well and latrine, and that there would be no end to this repairing and mending. But I also understood that our life is nothing other than such a repairing and mending: an attempt to keep in order an ageing body, declining memory, clothes wearing out and a home going to ruin, if one has a home. Life is just an endless work of repair.

✻

This old farmhouse is now home to my family and I. I have repaired most of the roofs, nailed soft insulation pasteboard and plywood on the walls, made new floors and put concrete curbs in the well. A man with an excavator dug a pond behind the sauna, and I planted about a hundred trees and shrubs on the previous owner's potato plot. The fastest-growing are the larches: some already overtop the roof; and the birches, oaks and pines are also tall enough for the children to climb. I've planted some exotic trees too. A few have grown well, for example the Lodgepole Pine, *Pinus contorta*, that comes from North America and differs from our pine primarily in that its needles, sprouts and even twigs are twisted. The Japanese Cork too was already a big tree when a cold winter damaged it. Most of its branches died; only a smaller one is still alive. Several other trees have suffered equally from the cold. The firs I like most are often hurt by roebucks who rub their antlers against the trees, stripping their bark: this is how they mark their territory. Sometimes they even attack oaks, linden trees and thujas, but these recover better from injuries.

✻

In Oslo we visited the Viking ship museum where, exhibited beside the restored ships, are many objects found in the Oseberg, Gokstad and Tune ships in which noblemen were buried. Nearly all these objects – the whole artificial environment of the ancient Nordic people – were made of wood: dishes, tubs, barrels, chairs, carriages, sleighs, dragon heads, beatles, cups, spoons, beds, houses... In a showcase of objects found in the Oseberg ship stood a round piece of wood of unknown purpose with a runic inscription, LITILIUSM, which should perhaps have been spelt LITILL VISS M – 'Little knows man' – although the interpretation is far from certain. On one vessel we saw the image of a small man sitting cross-legged; the vessel is called, jokingly, 'the Buddha-bucket'. Who knows, maybe this small man does indeed descend from Central Asia and that is also the place where Viking animal ornament has its roots. Then its model may well have been a Buddha-statue from this region, reinterpreted and recreated by a local craftsman.

❄

I was really impressed by the ships themselves. Their construction was so perfect that it couldn't have been bettered with the instruments and materials of the time. The Viking ships are Iron Age high-tech and it is no wonder that people in possession of them became rulers of nearly the whole of Europe, from Kiev to Ireland. One of my Norwegian friends told me there were Saamis among the men who built the ships. The Saamis were renowned as excellent boat-builders in some parts of Norway.

❄

I like thujas, although most of my friends don't. They think thujas are graveyard trees. For me they are first of all a North American tree, and one of several places I've felt very much at home was Vancouver on the Pacific coast of Canada. I felt this partly because I met plenty of these trees called cedars, as well as Douglas Firs, hemlocks, cypresses and firs, in America. All these trees have soft needles, and the oceanic air on the Pacific coast is soft and mild, so it was good to breathe and to be there. Breathing is nearly the same thing as being: this is something my contacts with Chinese taoists and books on their bodily exercises – *taiji* and *qigong* – have helped me to understand.

❋

In reality, this old farmhouse, this arboretum and garden are something more for me than just home. Actually I have many homes, I don't even know how many. I've tried to find them in several ways. One is with the help of trees. When I find a tree that I like, the place where it grows must be one of my homes. This is of course not only true of trees but of other plants as well, of the natural environment as a whole, of the landscape. In trees the spirit of the place, the genius loci, reveals itself with more clarity and force than in other plants, even in animals and people. Maybe with as much force as in stones.

❋

I feel that I definitely belong to an ecosystem, I have a place there, but I haven't yet found it, or have found only parts, fragments of it. I don't even know whether this ecosystem exists in the present world. Maybe it is extinct, maybe it is only a creation, a construction of my own fantasy, built up of plants, stones and landscapes that can never be found together in nature. Then looking for my home, my own ecosystem, is as strange a thing as planting this arboretum where an American larch, a Manzhurian walnut, a Caucasian *Pterocarya* and our own birch grow side by side. People often call the lowland birch Weeping Birch. Isn't it strange that even those who don't like thujas have no second thoughts about weeping birch trees, weeping elms and willows.

❋

My home, my arboretum, is an anthology of possible homes, a collection of places where I could feel at home, and it is possible that these places don't exist, have never existed. Some of them have been wiped out: the Ice Age, agriculture, desertification, mining or wars have completely destroyed them. Maybe I would feel most myself among plants that grew here in the Tertiary, in the Palaeocene when sequoias, gingkos and magnolias were common in Northern Europe. But I don't know, and probably never will. If it is true that time only flows forward. But what does 'time moving' mean, after all?

❉

The grasshoppers are cheeping and sawing. It's louder every night. Maybe I've begun to hear them more distinctly. More and more white moths fly against the window pane. Little white moths who come from darkness and return to darkness. In the wall, the death watch beetle ticks occasionally. Just like nineteen years ago when we came here for the first time.

❉

My poems and prose poems are also attempts to find a home, anthologies of existent and non-existent homes. If I were better acquainted with psychoanalysis, I would believe this comes from the fact that I lost my home as a little child and grew up in a flat shared by four or five families in the ruins of Tartu, and in the country at our relatives' homes. But in reality most Estonians are without a home and a homeland. They are emigrants, refugees, persecuted and taken for strangers even in the land that should and could be their homeland. For centuries we have been stepchildren in our father's home, kicked and scorned by a wicked stepmother, mocked and scoffed by her wicked children. This explains a lot, but not my passion for trees and stones.

❉

There's one more way of looking for your home: looking for plants, species, genera and families who behave like yourself, who have a predilection for the same sort of places as you. To look for your own family among those who got their names from Carolus Linnaeus. To identify yourself with plants, to consider yourself a plant or at least closely related to plants. And then to look at where its – that is your – relatives grow, what the landscape there is like, what people live there, what language they speak, what songs they sing. This is important too, although not as important as the plants themselves, the flora and the landscape.

❋

At other times and in other places people had soul animals, totems as they are often called: their relatives on the other side of the border we Christians and post-Christians have drawn between ourselves and other living things. I believe that we still have these relatives, that besides the genus *Homo* we belong to other genera, whether we admit it or not.

❋

It is possible that this is not a Linnaean relationship, that we are not so much related to a genus or a family, but to an ecosystem, a plant society or a life form. Maybe it means that we are related to the genius loci. In any case we do not belong, solely and sometimes not at all, to the place where we are born and grown up. Our citizenship, our origins and affinities, are much more complicated. We are citizens of the world, although this doesn't mean we are perfectly at home everywhere in the world. No, everyone of us has his/her own places and spirits of the place here and there. Some Estonians are spiritually more Native American, some are Hindu or Chinese, some are more Irish or French than Estonian. We are seldom able to find where our other homes are, even more seldom to visit them. Only now, as distant places become more accessible, can some lost children find their home. Even when there are several such homes, when they are scattered on other continents, islands and seas. That's probably the case with me.

❋

Maybe it's of some importance too that our stones and our sand come from abroad, from Fennoscandia. Our soil has been carried, floated, here from foreign lands; from foreign lands have we come, all the living beings on the Baltic shores. Strictly speaking men are not immigrants but natives only in Africa and possibly in Southern Asia. We arrived here just about ten thousand years ago, we colonised a land where the advancing glaciers had swept away all life, where even the soil had been pounded and the land itself flattened. People came back to the ruins of former landscapes where little by little new soil began to develop, and new plants appeared. The land, the landscape grew with the people. We have grown into this landscape, we cannot remember what was here before. We don't know among what ruins we've built our home. Sometimes this crosses my mind. It's odd to think about.

❄

In Alta, on a rocky hilltop, I saw clearly the tracks of a glacier. Probably the ice had pushed along a sharp piece of stone that had left these scratches. Similar ice-drawn lines can be found on limestone in some places in my country, Estonia. Their direction makes it possible to say which way the glaciers were moving here. That can also be guessed from the stones and boulders themselves. If we know where the type of mineral they consist of is to be found, we know from where the glacier broke them off and carried them here. These boulders are pieces, fragments of the ruins of Fennoscandia, the Fennoscandia of the Tertiary period, of sequoias and magnolias.

❄

When I flew from Britain to Canada for the first time, the Atlantic was covered by thick clouds, and to my great disappointment I couldn't see the ocean. I napped, then woke up and put on headphones where a Brandenburg Concerto by Bach was just playing. When I took a look down again, there were no more clouds to be seen, and the plane was just approaching the Labrador coast. Below us stretched a snowy landscape with frozen lakes, rivers, hills and forests. No trace of human habitation: no roads, no towns, no power lines. Neither the aborigine villages nor hunters' huts could be seen from the height of ten kilometres: I believe there were some below. On this virgin winter landscape I could distinguish – sometimes clearly, sometimes vaguely – lines running from Northwest to Southeast (I think this was the direction). These were furrows ploughed by the glacier, the valleys partly covered with lakes, the ridges with forest and bush. From the earth one can hardly discern the regularity of these drumlins and dales, but it becomes clear from a bird's eye view, from high above the ground.

❉

When the Germans retreated from North Norway, they evacuated the civilian population and burnt or dynamited all the houses, even buildings of the former observatory that had stood empty for a long time. When they had finally been defeated, the Norwegians and Saamis returned, built new homes and continue their lives nearly as before. Only slabs appeared on the walls of the churches bearing the names of people who had fallen in the war or been shot by the occupiers.

❉

Heather is the dominant species in heathland, heath forests and in drier bogs (especially in burnt-out places) and gives its name to corresponding forest and heath plant communities [....] On burnt-out places and clearings it reproduces itself easily with seeds; in shadow it has few flowers, the stems grow tall, and the plant can easily die out.
Flora of the Estonian SSR, vol. VIII, page 51

❉

This association (*Calluna vulgaris – Sphagnum fuscum + Rhynchospora – Scheuchzeria*) has developed as secondary as the result of burning (the domination of Calluna is the direct result of this). [...] Fire has probably favoured *Eriophorum vaginatum*, to a lesser degree *Ledum palustre*, which became abundant only two-three hundred years ago, apparently as a result of more intensive human activity.
Liivia Laasimer, Vegetation of the Estonian SSR, page 221

❉

The centre of Tartu had already suffered greatly in 1941, when all the bridges were blown up and the Soviet troops kept shelling the southern bank of Emajõgi from the northern bank which was still in their hands. A much more serious blow was dealt to the town in 1944 by massive bombardment by the Soviet air force. Then several historic blocks were destroyed, as well as many hotels, cafés, the former Treffner gymnasium, the 'Vanemuine' theatre and, among others, the house where we lived. When we returned to the burnt-out town, we found a temporary refuge with friends. Some china cups, plates and other smaller things had remained intact in our cellar.

✻

I was mowing behind where the cowshed used to be. Several toads crept away to hide from the scythe. Luckily they kept to the ground, lying flat between the tussocks. Sometimes I've hurt frogs and toads with the scythe. When they're hurt, they shriek. It seems that at the fear of death all shriek and scream the same way, a frog hurt with a scythe, a mouse caught by a buzzard, a hamster, a hare and probably a human being too. I have never heard the death scream of a man, but several of my acquaintances have.

✻

During the war the British and American bombers turned many German cities into ruin fields; for example the one in Dresden covered about eighteen square kilometres. In the centre of Cologne only the cathedral was left more or less intact, towering above the ruins. I've been told by a man in Cologne that among the people living in the cellars of destroyed houses the resistance movement gained a lot of support, and was quite efficient, so that high Nazi officials were afraid to show their faces among the ruins: some of them had been killed there.

✻

On the bomb sites vegetation soon appeared – communities of so-called ruderal plants – various weeds, grasses, shrubs and such trees as elder, aspen, willows, elms, maples and ash. Pine seedlings were found in the very centre of Berlin. More exotic species were represented by the butterfly bush (*Buddleia davidii*), which were quite numerous, and Ailanthus.

❈

I don't remember what plants grew in the deserted centre of Tartu. But one could certainly find willows, willowherb, birch, elder, maple and of course mugwort there.

Cf. Rolf Weber, Ruderalpflanzen und ihre Gesellschaften

❈

For several summers a little dark brown spider has nested under the lid of our well. I mean it has produced its young there. At first it guarded the cocoon full of eggs, then the tiny whitish spiders hatched out: in the beginning they were hustling in the cocoon and later they ran away in all directions. The spider doesn't seem bothered by the fact that the well lid is lifted many times during the day, and under its nest is a five metre deep hole with water in the bottom of it. I don't know whether it's the same spider or whether every summer a new one finds a nesting place under the well lid. If the latter either it was born and grew up there the previous year or it has found the place by special marks, a microclimate or the remains of cobweb. Under the same well lid, late every summer, I find orange moths. I even found their picture and name in an old German book about moths, but I can't recall the name nor find the book. When I draw water from the well, I usually throw them into the rose bush alongside, but next evening I find them under the lid again. Are these moths the same ones too or relatives of those I saw there last year? That's hard to believe. Most probably they simply like this shadowy, cool and protected place.

❈

After the war people in Tartu had to clear ruins in their free time. It was mandatory, and it had to be done with enthusiasm, with banners and slogans. It was called rebuilding, although only a few buildings were rebuilt: this was done by German POWs. Sometimes they were allowed to move around the town at large. They knocked at people's doors and asked for something to eat. Often they were given food, although the authorities didn't permit it. Most ruins were simply demolished and taken away. Parks were laid on the site of former blocks. Enterprising men gathered bricks from the ruins, cleaned them of mortar and plaster and built themselves little houses. It was the easiest way for an Estonian to get a home.

※

The heath family comprises about 40 genera with more than 1,400 species. The largest single genus is Erica: most of its species are distributed through Southern Africa, with some in the Mediterranean and Atlantic regions. These species are mostly xerophytes growing in open semi-arid areas. One of the species – the Cross-Leaved Heath (*Erica tetralix*) – is a characteristic of Atlantic heaths, and some scanty findings in Eastern Europe (in Latvia close to Liepaja, in Eastern Finland close to Kuhmo) suggest that it was more widespread in the past, probably in the Atlantic climate period. Most information about the species in Estonia is vague; it was found in a place near Haapsalu from where it had already disappeared by 1854.

※

Most heath plants of the Northern hemisphere are connected with the tundra or corresponding altitudes in the mountains. Ecologically most of them are xeromorphic oxylophytes which prefer shadowy, moist to wet sites. In the tundra and the mountains they also grow in open areas.

Flora of the Estonian SSR, vol. VIII, page 37

※

I'm standing on a bare hilltop. Underfoot are white rock, yellow, black and brown patches of lichen, fragments of a painting that will perhaps be ready before the next Ice Age. The painter has plenty of time: animals, people, clouds, summers and winters pass between him and the rock like morning mist.

※

This landscape leaves me wordless, nameless and without desires. I'm a man without qualities, nearly nothing, a pair of eyes and the longing to stay here, to decrease, to grow smaller, closer to rock and soil, to change into a low plant, a crowberry, a bearberry, a lichen, an inscription on rock, an inscription I still can't read, that is both a greeting and a farewell. Like the Saami *joik*, the song without words, without a beginning and an end, born here on the open hills under an open sky.

✱

I'm thinking of the seidas, those stones standing on hilltops which are often called *chorr* in the Saami language. These stones impersonate what I have called *genii loci* in this book. I think Christianity is agoraphobic: God got a home that was built as a fortification. In the early Middle Ages it was considered a castle where the forces of good and light could withstand a siege by the forces of evil and darkness. A Romanesque church was a bridgehead of the heavenly legions into this world ruled by Satan. Under the vast arctic sky of Lapland all this seems ridiculous and incomprehensible. How can people retire into their values, fears and beliefs like snails into their shells? How can one live in this world so egoistically, how is it possible to lose the sense of wonder, to live without noticing this sky, these white rocks, these crowberries, checkerberries, dwarf birch trees and diapensias? How is it possible to turn one's back on it all and build huge stone castles where there is art, music, colour, aroma and spirituality, where there are just no life and no light of men, no plantain and knotgrass, and of course no heath plants?

✱

My head aches slightly. It's been raining for several days. The air pressure seems to change. I often feel better with low than with high pressure. It's nice to breathe warm moist air. It was like that in Vancouver, it was like that in Canton on the South China Sea. The air there was amazingly light and this feeling of lightness is the background to my memories from South China. Even there I had a little time to botanise, to climb up to a bush growing on a hillside, to find bracken, honeysuckle, a pepper, a phylodendron and a wild rose with white flowers. The cuttings of the rose and pepper took root, and on my kitchen window sill I have a leguminous shrub that sprouted from a seed and has already grown a span. I couldn't find out its precise name.

❋

But my plants, my plant relatives in China, are probably not from the *Lonicera* or rose family, they are something else. I think I find them in the mountains among rhododendrons or conifers. In China you can find several rare and strange species of conifers such as metasequoia. But I have written about this tree before.

❋

On the southern slope (*yang*) of the promontory reaching into the fjord there is very little vegetation, only grass and crowberries. The northern slope (*yin*) is covered by a juniper thicket where even the dog gets about with difficulty. In the bushes one can see duck and seagull feathers. I take a feather and let it go in the wind from the hilltop. The wind carries it far away, then it abates and the feather begins falling, flutters to and fro, and finally lands on the bushes. On our way back we find the ruins of a German bunker: they even dynamited their bunkers before retreating. Rusty pieces of armature dangle like broken twigs from the concrete boulders. Here and there on the hills one can find scraps of barbed wire. In the war the German military outnumbered the locals here.

❋

The genus *Diapensia* belongs to the *Diapensiaceae* family and in the opinion of some botanists also to a subfamily, *Diapensiales*. Its best known representative *Diapensia lapponica*, is a characteristic species of arctic dwarf shrub tundras; here it is conspicuous for its flat or round mats. In unfavourable conditions the shrub grows very slowly: reaching flowering age at 5-10 years its circumference doesn't usually exceed 3-5 centimetres. *Diapensia lapponica* also grows in some isolated areas outside the arctic region, for example in Korea or in Scotland where it was discovered only twenty years ago: proof that even in countries which have been floristically as well studied as Britain it's possible to make important botanical discoveries.

Urania Pflanzenreich, Höhere Pflanzen 2, p. 169

✽

Some kilometres from our country home are an abandoned gravel pit and, close by, the Chapel of the Cross Lake. It is said that the lake was created when a church built here sank underground. The story goes like this: one Sunday when people had gathered for a service an old grey man came out of a large tree (it was probably a pine). He picked up a boulder, carried it into the church and put it on the floor. The church began to sink, but the people had time to run out before it vanished completely and water gathered in its place. I think this legendary place must have been a pre-Christian sanctuary on which a chapel was later built. The place is next to a crossroads, and crossroads had a special importance in ancient folk religion: our ancestors had certain secret rituals to be performed on a Thursday night at a crossroads.

✽

Sometimes we visit the gravel pit with our children. We gather interesting stones, bring home nice coarse sand that can be found in various places. The boys take tin cans and bottles left there by workmen, throw them in large pools of water and try to hit them with stones. Lately people have begin to use the gravel pit as an illegal waste disposal site. Digging for gravel some big boulders were exposed. One such boulder was brought to my courtyard by a friend of mine who was working on an excavator. I had painted a cross on it with white paint: so he could recognise it easily. Now the boulder stands under young larches: the white paint turned out to be very resistant and I couldn't scratch it off.

✽

In the beginning the gravel pit reminded me of a desert, especially one part, an expanse of sand with sparse little plants on it. Every year, more and more plants appear on the naked gravel and sand. Little by little bushes, too, make their appearance on the devastated land.

�֍

Across the bay from Alta there is a village called Kåfjord. In the middle of the past century a copper mine was founded there by the English. What remains of this copper mine are huge pits in the ground, huge heaps of slag and some slabs with foreign names in the local cemetery. For example:

THOMAS WILLIAM HOOKER TRENERY
DIED THE 1TH OF AUGUST 1838
AGED 3 YEARS

Happy Infant early Blest,
Rest in peaceful slumber, Rest.
Early rescued from the Cares
Which increase with growing Years.

The graves of the English and other more important people are next to the eastern wall of the church. There rests the early blest infant Thomas W.H. Trenery and a Swedish merchant Carl Johan Ruth, born in Luleå on July the 21st 1818 and died in Kautokeino on November 8th 1852.

�֍

Ruth also sold spirits to local people. This was one of the main reasons why he was killed by rebel Saamis from Kautokeino. For the murder two men, Aslak Haetta and Mons Somby, were sentenced to death, and were beheaded in Alta. Mons didn't regret what he had done: he said he knew God had forgiven him everything. Aslak panicked, he hoped until his last moment that he would be pardoned, and struggled desperately when he was dragged to the scaffold. The heads of both men were sent to the university anatomy chamber in Christiania where they are to this day. The bodies were buried in unconsecrated ground on the edge of the cemetery. In 1883 the writer Magdalene Theresen wrote that the two executed men rested beyond the churchyard 'in a gravemound given by Nature itself'. On this gravemound one can see plenty of shrubs, grasses and flowers, as proof 'that the earth is as good and kind everywhere, whether it carries a sign of blessing or not'.

※

The gravel pit is a desert: gravel roads and asphalt roads are deserts too, like town squares and streets. But even the field and the garden plot are deserts where for a short time we give some half-desert vegetation a chance to grow and bear fruit. It is more or less proven that the ancestors of present-day grains – wheat, rye, barley, millet and other annual grasses that don't store their supply of starch in the roots, but only in the seeds – originated in arid regions south of the glaciated areas. These plants germinate during the short moist winter and spring, grow up and bear fruit rapidly, and wither at the beginning of the dry period. Only the large seed-grains outlive this period. Images of the dying and resurrecting God were born in places where people began to cultivate such grasses. There Jesus could tell his parables about wheat and weeds, there he could say that if the grain didn't die, it would not bear fruit. Christianity is a cereal religion. Naturally people who subsist on hunting, fishing, gathering acorns, growing taro, manioc or coconuts, have a very different religion. To change these people into good Christians one should first plough up their land, change it into semi-desert. A religion has its own ecology, its demands on the environment like a tree or a shrub. Every religion and god belong to a specific landscape.

※

There is a theory that the Saamis are descendants of those people who survived the ice age on iceless mountains – *nunataks* – in Scandinavia. It could have been somewhere close to the sea where it was possible to hunt sea animals and to fish as the Chukchees and polar Eskimos do. These Eskimos could hardly survive if there were no *nunataks*. The word itself comes from the Eskimo language. There is, however a flaw in this theory: the preglacial inhabitants of Europe were not humans like us, but Neanderthal people who cannot have been the ancestors of any present-day group of men. But maybe the Saamis are the most direct descendants of those reindeer hunters and fishermen who followed the reindeer northwards occupying the territory vacated by retreating glaciers, the territory that was step by step changing into tundra, the first postglacial ecosystem here in Estonia too.

✻

Salix polaris – polar willow, height about 1 cm, leaves thick, without nerves.

Salix herbacea – grass willow, height up to 2 cm.

Salix reticulata – reticulate willow, height up to 5 cm.

Betula nana – dwarf birch, height up to 50 cm.

Diapensia lapponica – height up to 3 cm.

✻

Life contracts, keeps to the ground, creeps into fissures, into hollows where there is a handful of turfy soil and detritus; above it the wind, the midnight sun and some ants. Nearby some lichens are engaged in a silent world war – the black lichen conquers some territory from the yellow one, the yellow from the black.

✻

I think that what I want to say is hard, maybe even impossible, to express in human language and easier in the language of those odd plant names invented by somebody motivated by who knows what. *Salix, Calluna, Erica, Rhododendron, Diapensia, Loiseleuria, Cassiope, Empetrum, Andromeda...*

✻

The sun is still shining there beyond the Arctic Circle, on the hills of Alta. Here it's night, the wind has abated, two bats are circling above the pond, the great-tits have gone to sleep under the eaves of the children's hut. There are no curtains on the attic window, and the darkness is looking straight into the room. The darkness is like a huge black eye where I can still discern a reddish glow at the western horizon, and the reflection of my own face.

❄

If God's in his heaven, as they like to say, this is the faith of a desert people. Heaven – the sky – is a desert, a blue, black or grey desert. The sky is an unknown territory, as full of dangers as the desert where jackals, wolves or a band of robbers on a raid can suddenly appear.

❄

The sky is the home of an unknown and dangerous God, a desert of a God you can go to or turn your eyes to, if you have to be alone with yourself. Let's keep in mind that there are no borders in the sky just as there were until recently no borders in the desert between Chad and Libya or between Oman and Saudi Arabia. The borders you can find in the sky, the borders between clouds and constellations, are fuzzy and fast-changing, they are impossible to describe. Norbert Wiener has written about it in his book *Cybernetics*. The sky is like a desert, like a field. Can anything grow there? It could only be something fuzzy and contourless, something that's like clouds, light and rain.

❄

He who sows wind, reaps storm.

❄

In the forest close to our house is a place we call 'the burnt house'. Of the house itself little remains except foundations partly hidden by sorbaria bushes. There are still a few apple trees, already overgrown by the forest; some currant bushes, lilacs, linden trees and an elm. There's a story which is told about the destruction of the house in the late forties. From time to time the guerillas hiding in the forest, the 'Forest Fellows', came here to rest and have some food. Once, when they were right here, a mop up operation was launched and soldiers encircled the farm. One of the Forest Fellows lost his nerve and fired his gun from a window. The soldiers and militiamen answered with a barrage of fire. The house, hit by incendiary bullets, was soon in flames. The people still in the house tried to escape. The wounded woman of the house got out, but the soldiers caught her and threw her back in the flames: this is what people say. Nobody escaped. A son of the murdered woman was not at home at the time, he didn't know where to go. He was in hiding for a while at his neighbours', then joined the Forest Fellows to revenge his mother.

❄

Higher on the mountains the snow doesn't melt even in July. The forest keeps to the valleys and close to the sea where it is warmer. If you look at these landscapes from a plane the forest resembles crowberries, diapensias and dwarf birches creeping over the earth, seeking protection from the cold and wind. The people keep close to the forest, their houses stand close to it. In the North we human beings are like fleas living in fissures or in animal pelts. In Estonian they used to say that the forest is the poor man's fur coat. The forest is Earth's fur coat too, the same forest that is being destroyed at a fast pace, hundreds and thousands of hectares every day. That's how it is in the South, in Amazonia, in Zaire, in Borneo. The southern forest is made into toilet paper for the Americans, Australians and Japanese. Civilised man, the civilised flea, wipes his arse with the forest, wipes his arse on the fur coat of Amazonia, Borneo and Zaire, and throws it away.

※

We seldom look at the sky. You can do it most easily lying on your back. Then you discover that in the desert above us there are living beings: swifts, buzzards. When you look longer and more painstakingly you may even notice a star, most probably the Morning Star.

In reality the sky is just depth; it is distance, the third dimension. It is difficult to understand. Even when we know it, when we are well acquainted with the stars. This understanding has no limits: we can always have a deeper and clearer understanding of the depth of the sky.

When we have understood the depth of the sky we may begin to understand the depth of the fields, deserts, forests, or perhaps of ourselves. A field, a desert, every landscape is an echo of the sky and of its depth. We are an echo of an echo of the sky.

※

While speaking of the sky and of the desert I've forgotten the sea. But the sea didn't forget us. It began with our clothes, which we had left on the beach when we waded through the water to a tiny sandy islet. There we gathered some nice pebbles and shells. When we returned we noticed that the high tide had arrived. Jens' jacket with the car keys in its pockets was floating inland, Signe's shoes following. I'd put my own shoes higher up, and the sea hadn't yet reached them.

※

My home is first of all a landscape. Like this Observatory Hill on the fringe of Eurasia, in quiet midsummer Helsinki where I suddenly meet several friends such as *kaljo*, *kaie* and *kalle*: white clover, sparrows, honeysuckle and birches trying to grow in cracks in the rock. The rock itself is homely, reminding me of the half-dark kitchen, with a stone floor, from Eoste or Räpina.

❋

The same stone in us all. We are made of the same stone. Estonia too, because we live on what used to be the delta of ancient rivers that carried sand and clay here from the Fennoscandian mountains, and where later glaciers left boulders broken away from their stony laps.

❋

It's already completely dark. There are more and more insects flying around: I can't keep the window open when the lamp is lit, or there would soon be a swarm of large and small moths and craneflies. A cranefly came in from the loft. I caught it, turned off the lamp, opened the window and threw it out.

❋

The last Ice Age was a relatively recent event, here it ended about eleven thousand years ago, in the North even later than that. On Svalbard, in Greenland, and in the Antarctic, the Ice Age hasn't ended yet. In Siberia and the North of Canada the permafrost hasn't melted yet. And we don't know whether it will begin to melt or just the opposite: enlarge its area. We live in an age of disasters that have changed a large part of the continents into desert. The Antarctic and Greenland are ice deserts, the whole northern part of the temperate region is a taxonomic desert. We have lost most of our plant species, maybe even as much as 90% of them: the cedars, sequoias, araucarias, gingkos, magnolias, palms, sandalwood trees... Studying a book on paleobotany I discovered with astonishment that representatives of most tropical plant families grew here too before the Ice Age. Some of them retreated to the South, some died out. What is left to us is devastated land where we can find only the pitiful remnants of earlier forests, only a couple of species of tree instead of several hundred as we can still find in the South. I don't think that most people living in northern countries bother about it: they like spruce, birch and alder forests and meadows and find them homely. But I cannot forget what grew here once leaving behind only needles, twigs or pieces of bark encapsuled in amber. I know that this land is not fully my home without these extinct forests. It is as if our vegetation were trying to cover its poverty and absence of character with exuberant growth. Our grasses and trees are tramps, migrants like the brown rat and wolf. We lack our own vegetation. Even our plant societies are the poor man's meagre variants of real societies that have disappeared or retreated to lower latitudes far away from here.

※

The lilacs were in bloom some weeks ago, the pavement is covered with fallen guelder rose blossoms and a juneberry is full of small berries. Church bells are ringing somewhere in the city centre. The space is very open. Space, full of wind which blows wherever it pleases. *Pneuma pnei. Spiritus spirat.*

There is no wind in the church. *Spiritus* is here, on Observatory Hill. Spiritus is the wind carrying seagulls, the babble of a baby, the sound of the bells and the noise of passing cars.

A seagull is standing in front of me, looking at me first with one, then with the other eye. It picks some parasites from under its feathers, shrieks a couple of times and flies away.

※

As late as the Eocene, araucarias and yellow-wood grew in Europe and elsewhere in the Northern hemisphere. Later they spread to the Southern hemisphere and quickly became rare in the North. At that time pines were dominant in the Northern hemisphere, that's to say on Svalbard, Franz Joseph Land and in other Northern regions.

※

Conifers are important as a source of amber: according to the latest information the amber-producing species (most probably belonging to the genus *Pinus*) grew in the Tertiary in Scandinavia from where their remnants containing resin were carried to the 'amber beaches' of East Prussia.

❄

The landscape is still there. Landscapes do not disappear so easily. Even glaciers cannot obliterate them. Landscapes are like bones, skeletons: as people in the past believed, a skeleton can acquire new flesh, the bones of an animal can rise to a new life. Can our landscapes too rise, resuscitate, get back their fur coat: sequoias, cedars, cypresses, cinnamon trees? Will we be able to resuscitate vanished species, communities and fur coats? Leave alone vanished peoples? Couldn't genetic engineering one day create something similar to the prehistoric trees which once grew around the Baltic? We have little time left. Nowadays we are wiping out species faster than they are being born. Maybe in the next million years a new vegetation will develop on Earth. Yes, it's possible here in the Baltic region, but not on Svalbard, not on Franz Joseph Land. There the ice would have to disappear, the glaciers melt. But then the level of the oceans would rise, drowning the Netherlands, Denmark, West Siberia. The climatic zones would shift, the deserts would move northwards. Terrible famines would hit mankind, hundreds of millions would migrate. But must Svalbard then stay forever under ice? Can forests never grow on Greenland as in the past? I still think it might be reasonable to let the Earth warm up, the glaciers melt. Maybe we could rearrange life on Earth without glaciers. The Antarctic, Greenland and Svalbard would be colonised by those whose homeland was inundated by the sea. It is quite possible that this will happen, but I am afraid that it will happen as a disaster. Maybe the mission of the genus Homo is to introduce the postglacial age, but *Homo* is himself a child of the Ice Age, a child of the Snow Queen. Couldn't the Snow Queen take revenge on us for driving her away from our planet?

❉

Heath plants were among the first to return after the glaciers retreated, when the Snow Queen relaxed her grip, when the rocky and gravely earth became free of ice once more. Even now they are often the earliest and only ones. Like diapensias. They can grow in fissures and hollows where they find a little raw humus. *Empetrum, Cassiope, Arctostaphylos, Loiseleuria.* Even a rhododendron, the Lappish Rhododendron. Maybe some of them were able to resist the cold and escape the glaciers by retreating to the nunataks to survive the most difficult times of Snow Queen's rule, biding their time, as they can now too. Even in other places they can live on frontiers, frontiers of glaciers, deserts and civilisation. Rosebays in the Tibetan mountains, Ericas in the Cape wastelands, heather on burnt moorland.

❉

I don't know what it is that I like best about heath plants. It's as difficult to explain what features I love in people I do. In a sense it's all these features one by one – flowers, face, stalk, hands, modesty, smell, voice. The voice of a bumblebee on a heath flower. And then all this taken together. Man, heath, mountain top: I feel that we are somehow similar, that we have similar expectations, that we like one another's company. I like the company of heath plants and diapensias. I hope they like my company too. Probably I am somehow related to heath plants, maybe I belong to the heath family, to dwarf shrubs. Maybe I am related to diapensias. This doesn't match at all with modern taxonomy, but here recognition is more important than taxonomy.

❋

In fact trees and shrubs are a part of us, they are simply at a greater distance from our body than hands or feet, so it is possible to think that they don't feel pain, that chopping away our branches and trunks doesn't cause us serious injury. But we cannot live without trees. The fewer trees there are, the less we live. In reality we are chopping up and cutting down parts from our own body, we are burning and poisoning ourselves. Instead of the forest new human beings can be born, but they are disabled people, people without branches, without roots, without trees, without Amazonia, without Borneo, without Ruwenzori.

❋

In one of my most beautiful dreams – I have already written about it somewhere – I saw tall heather bushes in bloom on a faraway island. It was like a forest, a heather forest, and I could see the sky through the blossom. It was as if the sky were two-layered: the blue of the upper sky reached my eyes through the violet blossom of the lower one.

❋

If the sky is the Heaven some of us – as it is believed – will be taken to, can we find heather there? Is there a place for threatened and extinct trees, for sequoias, gingkos, cordaites? We are related to them: I am related to heather, somebody else to the gingko, a third one to the dwarf birch. We cannot leave them alone. We have a common destiny. I couldn't go to heaven, even if they wanted to take me there, without all these shrubs and trees, spirits, *genii loci*, birds, animals and fish. They are my relatives. I must take them all with me. I have given a promise, taken an oath.

❉

Perhaps we will all be sent to hell where we will burn in an everlasting fire, all of us, ferns, club mosses and cordaites, some of us as coal, some of us as we are now. Well, I am a sinner, even a poet, but why should horsetails, conifers, rhododendrons be punished? Why create and then fossilise all these wonderful beings? Are God's doings absurd or is our understanding of him or her and of his or her doings absurd? It's easier for me to believe in an absurd me than in an absurd God who is conducting horrible experiments in evolutionary biology on planet Earth. It's easier for me to place God in the end than in the beginning, to imagine him or her waiting for all of us, for all resurrected people, animals, birds, trees, shrubs, spirits, goblins and lichens.

❉

I know that the question 'why' is invalid outside our home, even more so in the areas of geology, cosmology and theology. In eternity the why-questions have no meaning at all. Like the questions about suffering, the causes of suffering and the way out of suffering. And I think that there is some eternity in the heather blossom – in its miniature twisted trunk, its tiny leathery leaves, in its huge kin, its acquaintances and friends, bees and bumblebees, wind and clouds – if we only take notice of it: it has the same colour and smell as our own eternity. Or perhaps – it may be more correct to say – it is as colourless and odourless as eternity.

❉

Pines grow beside our track; the soil beneath them is acid and poor: Sheep's Fescue, moss and even some lingonberry shrubs grow there. One autumn I planted some heather plants here. Now they have grown, multiplied and blossom abundantly.

✳

Maybe salvation and eternity are one and the same thing. Something looking at you from their blossoms. The rarer a thing is, the bigger its meaning. I think of this when I recall the tiny plants on the hilltops in Alta or three heather shrubs along our track under the pines. In our human vanity we believe in salvation somewhere in the depths of heaven or civilisation, in a desert that we have discovered or created. *Genius loci*, the spirit of place, the earth god, cannot find salvation without his or her place, without his or her spring, boulder or river. Stones and sand cannot find salvation without the mountains they come from, from where the waters have carried them here. I cannot find salvation without the heather, without the family of heath plants.

✳

The Buddha took a flower of Udambara and showed it to his students. They were not strong on botany and didn't understand. Kasyapa was the only one who recognised the flower, and understood what the Buddha wanted to say. He smiled. As to the Buddha himself, he was always smiling. Neither of them is here now, but the flower is here. Some sequoias and Bristlecone Pines that were young trees at that time are still here: the Bristlecone Pine can grow up to five thousand years old.

✳

It's August. The heather is in bloom. At the site of the burnt house there are apples on the apple trees. The grasshoppers are chirping more loudly from evening to evening. Some nuts are already falling from the hazel bushes. The rain has ceased, the swallows fly high. For a moment, the sun comes out from between the clouds.

Alta–Helsinki–Veskimõisa 1989

III

FROM
Summers and Springs

Springs and summers full of song and revolution.
The Popular Front, demonstrations and confrontations,
time that takes you away from yourself and your poetry
so that you see them as if from cosmic space,
a way of looking that changes everything into stars:
our Earth, you and me, Estonia and Eritrea,
blue anemones and the Pacific Ocean,
even the belief that you will write more poems. Something
that was breathing into you,
as May wind blows into a house
bringing smells of mown grass and dogs' barks:
this something has dissipated, become invisible
like stars in daylight. For quite a time I haven't
permitted myself to hope it would come back.
I know I am not free, I'm nothing without
this breathing, inspiration, wind that comes
through the window. Let God be free,
whether he exist or no. And then it comes
once again. At dusk in the countryside,
when I go to an outhouse, a little
white moth flies out of the door.
That's it, now. And the dusk around me
begins little by little to breathe words and syllables.

*

In the morning I was presented to President Mitterrand,
in the evening I weeded-out nettles under the currant bushes.
A lot happened in between; the ride from Tallinn to Tartu and to
    our country home
through the spring we had waited so long for,
and that came, as always, unexpectedly,
all at once changing serious greyish Estonia
into a primary school child's drawing in pale green,
into a play-landscape where mayflies, mayors and cars
are all somewhat tiny and ridiculous... In the evening
I saw the full moon rise above the alder grove. Two bats
circled over the courtyard. The President's hand
was soft and warm. As were his eyes
where fatigue was, in a curious way,
mingled with force, and depth with banality.
He had bottomless night eyes
with something mysterious in them
like the paths of moles underground
or the places where bats hibernate and sleep.

*

The radio's talking about the Tiananmen bloodbath.
It was three years ago. Just before that
I was there too: the square was empty, the sun shining.
At night it was freezing, but the city air
was full of dust. I don't know whether it came
from the Gobi desert or from building sites
in the city itself. At the other end of the square
huge cauldrons were boiling: a bowl of rice
with sauce and salad for less than a dollar.
I still remember its taste
as I remember young men whispering
in all the cities at the doors of all the hotels:
exchange money exchange money exchange change.

*

The sea doesn't want to make waves.
The wind doesn't want to blow.
Everything wants balance, peace
and seeking peace has no peace.
If you understand this, does it
change something? Can you be peaceful
even where there is no peace?
Is it a different kind of peace?
Questions all over again. Answers
are few, as always.
The wave goes up and down.
A flock of birds flies low to NNE.
This, too, is a wave. Thought is waves, too.

*

God has left us: I felt this clearly
loosening the earth around a rhubarb plant.
It was black and moist. I don't know where he is,
only a shelf full of sacred books remains of him,
a couple of wax candles, a prayer wheel and a little bell.
Coming back to the house I thought
there might still be something: the smell of lilac and honeysuckle.
Then suddenly I imagined a child's face
there, on the other side, in eternity
looking here, into time, regarding wide-eyed
our comings, goings and doings in this time-aquarium
under the light of the sun going down;
and falling asleep under a water-lily leaf
somewhere far away in the west.

*

The possibility of rain... If rain is possible
everything is possible: spinach, lettuce, radish and dill,
even carrots and potatoes, even black
and red currants, even swallows
above the pond where you can see
the reflection of the full moon, and bats flying.
The children finish playing badminton and go in.
There's a haze to the west. Little by little
the fatigue in my limbs changes to optimism. I dream
I borrow a plane to fly to Cologne.
I must go in too. The sky's nearly dark,
a half-moon shining through birch branches.
Suddenly I feel myself like an alchemist's retort
where all this – heat, boredom,
hope and new thoughts –
is melting into something strange, colourful and new.

*

A fit body doesn't exist. There are only space,
extension, endless possibilities,
the fact that you can touch that birch tree there,
fetch the big white stone from the ditch.
The sick body is everywhere: the room, courtyard,
path to the well, the house and the pale-blue sky
are all full of it. The sick body
is so big that everything touches,
hurts and injures it. A spruce branch swaying
at the fence comes in and bruises your face.
The wind swinging the witches' broom
blows through your breast.
The swallows' cries hit you like hammer blows.
Night falls like an old wet blanket on your eyes and mouth.

*

The age-old dream of mankind: to fly like a bird. A fairy tale come true not as a fairy tale but as a machine, an airline company that puts in motion lots of other machines: wheels, axes, levers and drives that sell you a ticket, ask SMOKING – NON-SMOKING, put you in a pigeonhole – BUSINESS CLASS, TOURIST CLASS, EUROCLASS, ECONOMY CLASS – and pack you into a huge cigar box in A, B, D, E or F, give you dinner, offer you cigarettes, earrings, watches, perfume and sweets. In business class drinks are free, elsewhere only the smiles and the air are free, but during the flight the air becomes denser and denser and you feel more and more of an urge to jump out, to break out of this cigar box, in order to really fly or at least fall into these white shining clouds, through which you can't see whether there is sea or land under you and on whose far edge another plane is creeping toward Frankfurt like a cockroach on a white wool blanket.

*

The city's humming, rumbling and buzzing,
turning around and hustling like an anthill on wheels:
a concrete mixer, the barrel slowly rotating
French, Africans, Khmers and Chinese,
one Estonian smoking at the window
and on the other side of the street a *clochard*, also smoking,
who's already been sitting for an hour on the doorstep,
outside the stream, alone
with his mongrel and three spotted pigeons
who always find something to peck at on the pavement.
I'd go to the Jardin de Luxembourg, but haven't the energy
to push my way through this spinning microcosm,
people, chairs and cars,
words, thoughts and sights
that will not vanish, but remain
like cobwebs floating in the thundery air
crumbling slowly on windowsills
and on the street, into somebody's bag,
into somebody's hair or a bouquet
that withers quickly in the heat.

*

The ship glides north. It's the only
sign, mark, on the boundary between sea and sky
that's vanishing into darkness and fog. Lighthouses, beacons,
each of them speaking with its own voiceless voice. The sea's
    breathing
in the rhythm of night waves. We breathe
in the same rhythm as the sea, we
fleas, bugs, parasites of the ancient sea,
fungi grown out of soil, who've now
spread our filaments into earth, wood and air.
I don't want to shut the window. I lie
with eyes open, thinking about the prints of birds
on wet sand and about Death, who once upon a time
road here in an old peasant carriage. I don't know
whether he or his carriage left prints
anywhere other than in dreams and legends.
If there were any, could we recognise them?
Could he recognise us?

*

The tide's low, and the sea has left lots of things behind: sea bottles, sea bags, sea boxes, seashells and jelly fish. Jellyfish remind you of bowls of jelly turned upside down on the sand. Empty open seashells are also silent, maybe even in Breton. They're old symbols, old vulvas which have lost their mystery, softness and darkness here in the cruel midday sun which demands you put on sunglasses and burns as intensely as if it wanted to leave of you, a Northerner, only a shadow on sand. You retreat, go back to the hotel with sore eyes. Your hands are salty when you taste them: maybe it's sweat, maybe the sea.

*

One day you will do everything for the last time: breathe, make love, drink, sleep and wake up. Maybe even think. One day you will visit Paris for the last time. If you knew when, you'd go somewhere you felt suited you. No, not to the Louvre, not to the Pantheon, not to a street café, not to a library, but to the botanical gardens, to the Jardin des Plantes where you have a chance to encounter the dandelion, wood sorrel and mallow who will acknowledge you. As you will be acknowledged by the silence that took you by the hand, helping you to overcome fear in your home on University Street in Tartu late one afternoon when everyone else was away. You were sitting on the sofa with a book in your hand. Darkness was falling. Distant voices changed their tone and the shadows crept out from under the wardrobes and beds. It's the same silence that was waiting for you in an old outhouse full of old wooden vessels and dust that nobody had cleaned up for years. The silence that took hold of you like a voiceless dark vortex dragging you into depths whose bottom you haven't yet reached. If there is any bottom at all: maybe there is only the echo, a rumble that has come nearer with every year, the deafening, dizzying TE DEUM or OM MANI PADME HUM of free fall, of freedom.

*

I was rinsing laundry at the pond when I noticed a small brownish butterfly had fallen into the dark water and was struggling there. The wind was pushing it little by little towards the bank. I followed the butterfly as people follow a competition: will it reach the bank before it falls prey to a water-measurer or a diving beetle surfaces and catches it? I was rooting for the butterfly, of course, but I didn't want to interfere with the course of Nature by helping it ashore. The wind was pushing it towards land, tiny insects were bustling around it. Then the butterfly reached a small hummock standing out of the water. But the breeze didn't bring it onto the hummock: it turned around it helplessly. Even getting to the grass would scarcely have saved it: the piece of turf was only millimetres above the water and ripples often went over it. Then I lost patience. I took a long horsetail and extended it to the butterfly: it clung on, I lifted it ashore and put it down on the grass.

*

Evening's coming. The land and the forest meet
the big cool silence that is disturbed
only by the buzz of gnats and the warning cry of a nightingale
from the bushes near our sauna. I come back from the garden
through chill alternating with warmth: it reminds me
of summers in childhood when I cycled
through similar waves of cold and warmth,
through the smell of pine trees and strawberries. Childhood.
No, I'd never like to get it back.
There was a shadow lying on my childhood. I have always
fled this shadow, am fleeing it even now,
although I feel that when I'm finally out of its reach
there will be only a void, a cool voiceless void
with pine bark peelings, feathers and ourselves
caught in a dizzying vortex, a free fall
from night to morning, from morning to night.

*

It's raining again, and Estonia is cooling like a sauna, like a fireplace. The rain is cold. Big drops fall from the balcony onto the window box that stayed empty this summer. Grandmother was too weak to grow flowers in the box as she had done every year, and she complained more and more. This summer she spent a couple of weeks in the countryside at her cousin's, she even wrote us a letter from there, but then we got a message that she had fallen very ill. She was taken to the hospital in town, and they found she had a large intestinal cancer. She never recovered from surgery but lived some days in a high fever, in a mental twilight, speaking in a loud voice to her dead relatives as if they'd come to take her. Maybe they really had, maybe she saw something we couldn't see. But we could never ask her about that.

*

The centre of the world is here, in Manchester.
I carry it with me
as we all do. The centre of the world
pierces me, the way a pin
pierces the body of an insect.
The centre of the world
is the pain.

*

The clay god wants to come back to the scene of history.

He never smiles. Nobody must see that his teeth too are made of clay, thus even his smile is a clay smile. And his tears would be tears of clay but he can't weep, the tears would melt furrows into his face and chest. He feels safer in times of drought and bitter cold when the air is dry. When it's raining or thaws he doesn't go out. He's afraid of water but not fire. In fire he can become harder and more ruthless, more god-like. I prefer the wooden god. He's born of air, sun and water. He is afraid of fire: in fire he burns, dissolves into air and water, maybe even into sun: we can't be sure about that.

*

A cloudy afternoon in late autumn. We're driving over a viaduct, the car shakes a couple of times going over the joins. It's sultry and misty. Soon it'll be getting dark. Suddenly I see snowflakes, one after another, falling on the windscreen. I'm as happy as if I'd seen a miracle. In a sense it is a miracle, although we'll have no real snow either here or in the countryside, where we'll arrive in half an hour bringing home apples and carrots. The feeling of a miracle having taken place will be with me on my way to our country home and back to town, and it won't vanish even in the petty doings of tomorrow; maybe only in the Parliament, though perhaps something of it will remain. Maybe it's a vision, as if a little god were pricking a pin through a grey condom put on reality by another, old and sulky god. Now there's a hole in the condom, and through the hole we can see something that could be a distant star or a spermatozoid glowing in distant light.

*

My poems often aren't poems; they're parts of a long declaration of love to the world, a long poetic list of people and things I love. When I was young I was fond of my thoughts, my feelings, my longing and joy. I approached the world like a hot air balloon which covered everything up. With the years the balloon has cooled down, shrunk, and I see more and more of other things, I see simply what is. This *simply what is* has always seemed odd to me. Sometimes I experience this oddity as elevated, sometimes it's simply funny. The feeling of oddity has never disappeared. It's probably deeper and more self-conscious than ever.

The wall clock was made in Valga in 1902, and it's still going quite well. It could even strike, if I had a chain for the other weight. But I don't believe I could get accustomed to a wall clock that struck hours. Now it's showing 11. It's December 31st, 1992. As often before, I am writing something in the last hour of the year. I'm not sure I would like to call it a poem. It's not taking much time, and the emotional atmosphere of the last hour of the year suits writing well. The tick-tock of the old clock suits this atmosphere well too. I think that maybe the dead clockmaker from Valga is sending his greetings to me and my family this way. I can't do the same to him.

*

Less and less space for flying. I don't know whether my wings have grown longer or the walls and ceiling of this room have shrunk, so that my left wing nearly touches the wall to my left and my right wing the wall to my right. When I rise a little my head touches the ceiling and my hair get chalky. It's good that I have grey hair, otherwise a glance at my head would show how little space I have left. At the moment you can probably only see it from my eyes, but it's not our custom to look into the eyes of other people, especially on New Year's Eve when all the cats and all eyes are grey in the same way.

*

There are animals who mark their tracks and territories with urine: mice, dogs and cats. Probably the smell of urine isn't disgusting to them. As it probably is to us humans: we are a different kind of animal. We are animals who don't want to step on the tracks marked by others or to recognise frontiers marked by others. Maybe our need to discover and create something new is simply a result of our revulsion at the smells of urine and sweat and an urge to change our shelters all the time. We're nomads by blood: our real home would be a hut woven of leaves with a fire burning in front of it. We spend the night under such cover in order to go on next morning, to go on to places where no foot has yet stepped, no thought yet reached, to places where there's still no smell of man, only the smells of flowing water, flowers, birds and moist earth. Maybe it really has been like that. Maybe what I'm writing here comes from an ancient tropical memory living in our genes, in the depths of our brain, something that has happened so many times that it cannot simply disappear. A hut woven of leaves under a huge tree, the chirping and shrieking of night birds and insects, night wind in the tree tops high above us, a bunch of half-naked people, some sleeping children. Somebody humming a wordless song. Somewhere in the north far from us the glaciers are advancing, but we don't know it. We don't know what ice looks like and we don't know much about the sea either. We've heard of the big bitter water where some fish are as big as several elephants, and some are small but they can fly. Now and then we tell our children stories of these strange fish and this bitter water, as our parents and grandparents told us.

*

More and more empty words, the tricolour under grey clouds, music, new ways of saying and doing things. You bow, smile, thank, ask questions, vote. But deep inside you a little child's voice is shouting louder and louder: 'How did I get here?'

Is this your home or a place of punishment, an alien bleak piece of land set against an alien bleak sea, an alien language and alien people to whom you must return again and again from dreams where you could be on these islands or in China, in Greece, in the West Coast cedar forests? We bow, we smile, we thank, we ask questions. The phone rings, you're caught by the phone line like a fish by a hook. Was it you somebody wanted to catch or are you just bait for somebody bigger and more important who lives here, on this bleak land in this bleak sea, and who is lured out of the depths by your story, your poem or simply by your despair?

*

The year's half over. In the room downstairs
the radio's playing rock music.
The vacation has arrived. For half a year
I thought: in the summer I'll write poems. Now
I'm sitting here and once again
the white moth comes into my mind.
The moth flew around the birch tree last night
and I felt I could write a poem about it; I felt
that what I would write about this evening,
this birch and this moth,
would be a poem. Maybe the moth
was just a sign, a sign of something
far away, higher and deeper,
as it has been a couple of times before. A signal:
somebody has escaped, takes wing,
flies away.
Branches swaying in night wind. A poem.
Come. Gone.

*

I saw something white far away at the roadside. At first I took it for a bike, then I realised that it was just a bunch of white *umbelliferae*. All morning I'd tried to read a poem by Ruan Ji, but with little success. There were too many words there meaning sadness, sorrow, pain and trouble. It seems there are dozens of such words in Chinese: this certainly means that the Chinese had a sophisticated culture of mourning and grieving. Early in the day the sun was shining, then grey clouds began rising from the north and it got chilly, with drizzle from time to time. I felt nearly as sad as the Chinese poet who lived 1,700 years ago. But I know from my own experience that a certain kind of sadness is connected with the birth or rebirth of your poetic gift. It's painful: poems aren't born easily, they always break something in you, rip you apart, take away a piece of your flesh, leaving a scar like those you got falling off your bike on a stony road or cutting your finger with a knife.

*

The weather changed overnight. The clouds that were like grey wolves changed into white sheep, creeping innocently up from behind the spruce hedge that leads to the neighbour's oat field. The granary roof which had turned nearly black with rain dried out and became light grey again. I wanted to do nothing but simply to be and to walk around in the midst of this summer which had finally arrived. We always feel it's too short, we have too little of it. Everything is suddenly clearer, is open, turned outwards, towards others, towards the clouds, towards light. I stood on the jetty, closed my eyes and listened to the voices of summer: the forest was murmuring, aspen leaves were rustling, and a late finch was singing in the alder grove. A school of tiny carp swam in the pond and a frog was quacking on the bank. I thought that I would like to be like these frogs: I would lie half the day in water and croak now and then. But one thought wouldn't let me go. A summer thought, a summer poem, was striving, was climbing higher and higher, believing that it would soon reach a surface, a wall. A thought that summer is like a huge glass bell around us and above us, catching all our voices and giving them a clearer sound.

Summer is a piece of our phylogenetic childhood that we carry with us as a deep dim memory. We don't go back to Africa where we come from, as swallows and storks do. But once a year Africa comes here, meets us here. Summer comes to us like a great psychoanalyst, a phylogenetic Freud. It's like a great wizard, it makes wonderful things: teaches fledglings to fly, transforms newts into real frogs and the meadow into a huge flowerbed. On some still, worm mornings it can even transform us into something more human. I dare not say whether it means we become more ourselves. But on a mild summer evening it means a great deal.

*

My eyesight's weakening. I don't see the plants in the lawn beneath my feet as sharply as before. And I always have the feeling that I haven't seen them enough. I would like to look, to see them with more reality, more in-depth; to look this patch of lawn, these knot-grasses, this clover, these *Alchemillas*, these *Plantagos*, these dandelions into myself. Or to look myself into them, to be for a while a stem of grass, a winding stem of vetch, a white clover blossom bending under the weight of a black bumblebee. I think I am simply afraid. I'm afraid that I still don't see all this with enough reality, so that I could take a patch of the lawn with me into the time when my eyes will see no more. In fact, I would like to take something of all this Over There, to the other side. I am afraid that, once there, I will have little left other than words: sentences and thoughts but no leaves of grass, no patch of lawn with dead oak leaves from last summer, no bumble bee in flight and no chirping of grasshoppers announcing midsummer.

I have gone through this world like a tourist through a museum. I've tried to glean something from these thousands of displays, to keep something essential in mind. But after visiting time is over, when the warden says that the museum is closing, there will be hopelessly little that I can remember. And lying there in an empty hotel room I'll think that during my whole life I have been unhappily in love with this wonderful world we have to hurry through. It's because of this unhappy love I want to get something of my own, to buy something really belonging to myself, as a man unable to win the love of a woman tries to turn her into his possession. But he too will finally have only an empty room and a memory where the words, sentences and thoughts have eaten up, forced out all the clover blossoms, Althaea leaves and the chirping of the first grasshoppers, where his eyes cannot recall the flowering of white clover or that curve of female hips he hoped was a gateway to another, more real world.

*

The world is a single event.
Events have no beginning and no end.
The wind moves the oak leaves,
the oak leaves move in the wind.
In fact there's no border
between the oak leaves and the wind,
no difference between the wind and the leaves and twigs
it moves, between the wind and this windy day
where the weather's changing, and for an instant
you understand the oneness of the leaves and the wind,
and a little green beetle
tumbles from the oak into your hair.

*

Through morning dreams, morning haze,
the raindrops drumming on the shutters
and the cock-a-doodle-doo of a rooster in the next street
touch the very bottom of your memory,
recalling the warm mornings of your childhood.
Eternity has many shapes and voice.
From time to time it reminds you of itself
in a raindrop, a cock-a-doodle-doo or the lilac aroma
between dreaming and waking between two dreams:
and what we call space and time
suddenly lose their meaning, turn into a rooster's crow
or a stream glimmering in morning sun
and vanish as haze vanishes in daylight
and night dreams in daydreams.

*

I opened the Russian-Chinese dictionary:
there between two pages was a tiny insect.
It spread its wings and flew away.
I lost sight of it, maybe
it's still struggling on the window pane
or has died there like so many insects or succeeded
in getting out into the open. Like some of us.
For a while I wondered if it couldn't have been
a word, a sign from the dictionary
which had had enough and wanted to become
something else, something more than a sign,
a hieroglyph under the cold glass covers
of this world, of this life.

*

It could have been thus. Yesterday
a million and a half years ago
far in the south an ancestor
halted on a dry slope
and suddenly heard in the chirping of the grasshoppers
a little voice that burst the closed space
both inside and outside him.
The animal fell apart, and the naked ape
who didn't yet know it was a human being
looked around, and understood that something
had changed. It understood
that it had understood something,
although for a million and a half years
it has been unable to explain it to others.

*

I've thought that I thought about death, but in fact I don't know how one should think of death. Death is probably very hard, as hard as life, but life is something you live piece by piece, whereas you die once and for all... Once and for all you have to tear away all the lived life – seven, seventeen, seventy, and if someone is very strong, eighty years – and to let them fall into an abyss, into the void. A tiny pale bodiless soulless somebody lingers for moment on the rim of the abyss. This is the one who has thrown away his life; it would be better to say he has let it loose. Seen from the other side life is death, life and death are one and the same thing. Life is something you must keep and guard all the time like a rat in a cage. Because it is so hard to think of death, I prefer to think of the currants: black, red and white currants which are so ripe that they fall when you touch the bush.

*

Suddenly, everything silent. No leaves stirring,
not even flies buzzing around you.
A lonely swallow high overhead.
The clouds have dispersed, fled behind the horizon.
I read old Chinese songs half the day,
then we gathered the dry hay into stacks. I'm standing on the stairs
watching and hearing how colours
begin to change in the silence: the blue
gets darker and deeper,
the yellow gets brighter, lights up, as it were afraid
that it cannot survive the approaching night.
I'm looking at this all with the eyes of long-dead poets,
and speaking with their words.

*

Tallinn is cold as the whole of Estonia.
I put on warm underwear, woollen socks
and a heavy Irish sweater.
With a numb hand I try to write,
giving myself consolation: the heart's still warm
and abroad they say warm words
about the Estonian economy and its future.
When will these warm words reach
the people who are too poor to buy meat,
to buy an electric heater and pay for hot water?
Thought moves sluggishly
like a lizard in a frosty morning
or an autumn fly on the north window.
We go shivering towards the rosy future
together with late lizards and flies,
with new Kurdish refugees,
their unborn babies and their poems
somewhere in a past or future prison.

*

I don't have a land or a sky of my own.
I only have a little white cloud
which I met once, as a schoolboy
lying in the courtyard on a pile of twigs
looking into the sky. There were martins
and clouds: this one, my only one, too.
I would recognise it today too,
through all the transformations,
if only I had time just to lie there
idly on a pile of twigs in the courtyard.

*

The whole town is covered with ice: streets, trees, cars, stairway handrails, lanterns. The footprints that people left on the paths in the park a couple of days ago, when it was still warm, are covered with ice too. If there's no big thaw the footprints will stay there for a long time, maybe even until spring. Maybe they will outlive some people who left them there in wet snow or mud. When it thaws the footprints will spread, get less distinct, but won't vanish completely. Now they aren't footprints of concrete people, but the footprints of mankind telling us of liberty, fraternity and equality. Free, fraternal and equal they will remain under the snow and melt and vanish only in spring. The water flowing in a gutter or evaporating in sunshine knows and remembers nothing of them.

*